The Palindrome of the Sun

poems by

Veronica Sanitate

Finishing Line Press
Georgetown, Kentucky

The Palindrome of the Sun

ACKNOWLEDGMENTS

"Reprise" was published previously in The Paddock Review.

I offer my deep thanks to my Stonecoast MFA mentor, friend, and advisor Katherine
Larson, who consistently championed my work, with particular attention to the
Palindrome section of my book Sun Standing Still, which was short-listed for the 2024
Faulkner-Wisdom prize.

And my vast appreciation to my husband, Bill Middleton, who has loved and supported
me from the beginning, and our children and children's children who've contributed so
much joy to our lives.

Publisher: Leah Huete de Maines
Editor: Christen Kincaid
Cover Art: Veronica Sanitate
Author Photo: Rachel Rane
Cover Design: Elizabeth Maines McCleavy

Order online: www.finishinglinepress.com
also available on amazon.com

Author inquiries and mail orders:
Finishing Line Press
PO Box 1626
Georgetown, Kentucky 40324
USA

Contents

There is no top or bottom, no absolute positioning in space. There are only positions that are relative to the others. There is an incessant change in the relative positions throughout the universe and the observer is always at the centre.

—Giordano Bruno

History Dries in the Medici Hills

While we nap, history grows thin, slips in through windows on the rim
of huge gusts; on rain that draws its indifferent hand through ancient
scripts disguising luck and origin. It saturates covers, dulls awakening,

mutes dreams, mutates time, as full summer arrives. Foot-thick walls signify
our villa as fortress—a fifteenth-century Medici outpost—midway
between Firenze and Pisa. In World War II, battles sprawled in the landscape

as if the place would never elude its original commission. But the Germans
could conquer only so much. In the hills, some stone homes coved
along winding roads were spared. Life went on unaffected.

The rain-soaked sheets are drying in the kitchen near the ancient hearth,
hearth so directly related to heart; see the centuries women pour
themselves into *zupe e pasta*. My father's and mother's grandmothers and

before, shaping dough into honest loaves, placing them in the small pocket
toward the back—the bread oven—where they transformed into pane, meta-
phor for fire, sustenance, continuity from ancestors to descendants.

Home's heart, the fire so ferocious it fastened to the stone, accumulating
and solidifying a black cinder coat fostered through generations. The wettest
of the coverlet's blotches now merely damp—the moisture amortized

in a kind of osmosis between present and past. Life does this. Even
in the damp air, an equalizing occurs. The sun shines even as it rains.
In France, great flooding today with loss of life.

Solstice: The Half Year Begins

At our villa at *Poggio Nardini*, every morning
I open wide the casement window to see
what's changed. I lean out, echo the sun-bowing
of a thousand morning men and women who look
for something, even disorder, in the orderly rows
of vines, olives, and lives sprawling through the hollows.

Nothing's changed—just the angle of light that
informs the leaves to grow, sheltering the vines' gilded
cargo. But change is invisible. It will be weeks before
we see the sun has shifted. Sun-filled bowls of grapes
will be our breakfast, sumptuous olives for supper, pressed
into oil for winter. Scarlet fruits crushed into jams and nectars,

but these are future. The grapes have not yet reached
veraison, the truing into purple when ripening
begins, then deepens in late summer. Then, harvest.
Then the forgetting.

> *En giro torte sol ciclos*
> the sun turns
> the sun stands still.

Grow now, mid-year children. Summer
begins. The year's half gone. The longest
day is here. The only day is now.

Bridge

Humans, standing in time, waiting on line for entrance
to a commitment from centuries ago. Time, a connective
arrow, whistles through; builds a tentative bridge. But one
must wait in line to enter . . . life, or the Gates of Paradise—

the Baptistery, based on a concept of temple when gods
were less subtle: *Noah, build an ark!* Days go on. Sunrises
duplicate, flow scarlet into sky above daylight. Persons
display who they are in what they create. When thought

changes enough, reconstruct the edifice. Look, you there,
near the precipice—look for what never shows—the evidence,
white rose of grief, joy's fleur-de-lis—but you, ahead in line,
await the guide. The third century temple recognized by

its wrecked foundation. The present borrows from what
went before. Think Pompeii's timeless embrace. The airless
rubble. Time eliminates breath, laminates death. But does
love persevere? Silence. On the wall: Kilroy was here.

The Palindrome of the Sun

i. In Italy, One Is Never in the Present Century

In the Baptistery, time backs us into the 11th century
when Strozzo Strozzi, astronomer and master, designed
on its floor a zodiac in intricate black and white marble.
Through an opening in the dome, the sun pinned
the time of year, a sundial, pacing through astrology's
symbols. In the center of the design—the sun.

Heliocentric—sun in the center—the "heresy"
for which, 500 years later, Galileo was arrested.
Clearly, over time, knowledge had deflected.
We lost time, abandoned *gnosis*—knowing
through observation and experience.

And here was Strozzi's masterpiece: When sunlight
struck through the center sun, solstice had begun.

How stunning it must've been to see
the sun light the floor's astrology;
the zodiac revealing month and time,
our place in the universe,
the nature of our souls and minds.
But to what avail? Knowledge and art
can't keep us. Strozzi was interred
under his own design;
his bones are dust;
the circle completes itself.

ii. The Sun Solidifies

blinds the eye of the marble statue
that looks like my son—wide-set eyes, nose
aquiline—had we been here in an earlier
time, in alternate cells of selves?

Outside the Palazzo Vecchio, Michelangelo's David
poised to sling his stone—formidable, but not entirely
fearless; in his frozen gaze, any mother can see this.

Time climbs its illusory line from sun up to down
and around the blue world, day, week, year, until
time, failed tide, retreats and light reverses.

It's solstice. The year's half done.

The Gates of Paradise are closed.
Their bronze reburnished, their fables
refurbished: Noah's drunk and Goliath slain.
Look elsewhere for salvation.

iii. Turned by Fire

In the Baptistery, an inscription in archaic Latin
circles Strozzi's sun. A palindrome, it can be read
from its beginning or end, like the sun's circular
movement and its turning back at the solstice:
En giro torte sol ciclos et rotor igne.

Sol in the center. I turn toward my friend who is
terminally ill. I want to say something meaningful
about life's circularity, summer's apex, the burning
and decline, but I grow lightheaded recalling
the aftermath of my childhood in Detroit. At fourteen,
while making tea, my robe caught fire, the flames
swarmed like a nest of furious hornets, searing
my back with their sting. My father beat the blaze
out with his hand—this was the week before
my mother, declining for years, died of cancer.

Sun gone then. Sun and its fire. Blaze and death.
Orange flame to depleted gray. Animus into
absence. Fire: element that conquers wood,

wind, water. And flesh. Then, where do we find
ourselves, my friend, and to what do we commit?

Is there a soul? Does it keep its fire?

But she is ahead of me, feeling her illness,

already near the gate that releases us.

iv. Palindrome of the Sun

Strozzo's inscription around the sun, clever
palindrome, a popular art of the time, barely
legible now. Here, the form mimicked the sun's
ecliptic and its seeming back and forth journey.
In the engraved design, when light aligned
as a gnomon through the center of the sun,
solstice had begun. You could trace it from
its beginning or end as it retreated through time
until spring rose again.

En giro torte sol ciclos et rotor igne

The exact translation from Medieval Latin is unknown.
I offer my own:

I, the sun, spin the spheres in circles and I am turned by fire.

The words, read in reverse, point to a similar
universe, reading backwards, something like:

Turning by fire, I, the sun, spin the circles

Reading this way, the concept of "spinning
circles" emerges—because though the letters
are the same, the words are different.

Engi rotor te solcic los etrot orig ne

But the letters, recombined to match the number
of letters in each of the words going forward,
make the palindrome perfect. This form is called
a "rotor"—meaning "wheel"—*rotor* being

a palindrome itself, appearing in the middle of

this palindrome. To see it more clearly:

En gi ro tor te sol cic los et rot or ig ne

My final:

In twisted spinning, I, the sun, rotate the circles
and I turn by fire.

The sun is the center of the galaxy.

Sometimes knowledge is lost.

Because who would *not* want to believe

the earth—and man—are in the center

and in control of the universe?

v. Still, I Mean to Decipher

The guide's words come back to me—no translation for
the ancient Latin. "Lo! I turn twistedly," began one try.

In the rotunda, French, Italian, German dialects
splash in air like a Romanesque fountain. The guides,
effervescent, reveal recent excavations. We peer
downward through glass, falling under time, beneath
spines and centuries: *this wall of ruins from first century*
Romans; this from the third, a temple to Mars—the Baptistery
renewed in 1059, rededicated to St. John, even now
being rebuilt. God is steadier now, though a shiny reclining
effigy honors deposed Pope John XXIII, one of four
who claimed the papacy. Remember Avignon? Lavender
fields, the bridge we sang about in French class
(Sur le pont), the Palace of the Popes *(Palais des Papes)*.

They digressed, as I do. It's not just the words
"*En giro torte...*" I mean to decrypt. It's life, its fire,
its orbits. The marble design at the north door was
removed centuries ago. The sun no longer staggers
through Strozzi's design. We've lost time, or are
lost in it, can't complete our thought. The Zodiac
was moved more than once; today, rests—an oddly
situated mosaic—in a Byzantine floor enclosed

by ropes designed to protect the ancient stones
and keep the modern out.

But seemingly for centuries, one could simply step on stars
and sun, the sun twirling with fire, whirling its planets
around. And you and I speak as if this is ordinary. Not
just standing on stars—the part where, without a hair
out of place, we zip around the sun at 67,000 miles an hour,
spinning a thousand miles per hour like a top.

vi.   The Sun Stands Still

Solstice: sol—sun, and *sistere*—standing still

We track the sun, our visible god.
But its daily movement through time
is as imperceptible as the growth of trees.
During solstice, the sun seems to stand
still for three days—
one day reaching its zenith over the Tropic of Cancer,
then resting,
then beginning its retreat.
The word "tropic" from the Greek "tropikos,"
which means "turn," refers to the sun
turning back at solstice—like a palindrome.

In the 11th century, one could watch sunlight
pour through an opening in the dome. Follow
as it shifted like indecipherable music
through the zodiac carved in the Baptistery
floor. Because of how the constellations aligned
back then, you would observe the sun leave Gemini.
Enter Cancer.

vii. Strozzo Strozzi's Song

You wouldn't have heard it at all had the Zodiac
not been removed from the floor. As if shifting

the stars unsealed his tomb, admitting time
to admix dust with return. Rebirth for this place

of Baptism. Temple eternally being reformed. Song
not the blues you or I would sing. More a whistle and hum

of wind. A bit of storm that startles with metallic edge,
scent of lead; a note flies by just as you notice—

like a bullet that misses but grazes your head. Still, a song
we were born for—doesn't end; continues through seasons

of river and wood, light, a light chant like the song
the forest people would sing naming the boulders

and rivers they passed to mark their passage and find
their way back. It's receivable only as breeze;

higher than mind can read. A scent: an eternity of fleur-de-lis
in stagnant bliss—even a tomb door can't interrupt this.

I know you are asking—the wave of your question
arrives like an aria from the now of your reading

to the Renaissance then of my listening, echoing back
to the monophonic chant of the 11th century . . .

What was Strozzo singing? And I think you mean beyond
the continuity which can't elude us, his work still with us . . .

He is saying with emphasis and in earnest: *stars!* We are
from the stars, ad astra and thus, connected to the constellations . . .
which I have managed, he says with a dollop of pride,
to capture and place on the floor from the sky . . .

    I sing the "*ah*" of creation.

viii.   The Internal Weeping

Stony as statuary we are. Italy itself suggested it,
coldly blending the proportions of Vitruvian
Man and the golden ratio, internally reflecting
the golden mean, which has to do with balance.

Who were we then? Who are we?

As if we uncovered a crypt and the body was gone,
we intuited this: that we might've lived before
and might again after this. We wept at this,
fragile though the evidence.

Are we jade weed of contained self, solid as stone
yet internally liquid? The green fuse of us contained
in its own sphere, yet flowing, flowering, becoming
and dissolving into its spiral, fluid as hourglass sand,
elements solid—like lead—but embodying permeability,
as if statuary like David were real, were somehow

Michelangelo himself, and you and I could begin . . .

to absorb this identity—artists and art; God and story;
statue and human; tree, breeze, atom, Adam. Charmed,
alarmed, weep. River Arno its own vehicle with its own

traffic, but inhabits us as thought, fractions, fractals,

a foundation that rearranges and reassembles into air

earth fire and nothing but flow—

still, must we go?

ix.   *Watching Time Pass*

Since Strozzi, a thousand summer solstices have slipped

through the Baptistery edifices leaving only a thin

beam of continuance. My son and I stroll

to the Palazzo Strozzi, now a museum, fascinated

that some names, their buildings and works

have withstood centuries. We know it's what

art does, but what of the rest of us? What of us?

Even the Medici are now heirless and Strozzo

himself hard to find.

We enter the Palazzo to see De Chirico's 1912 painting,

"The Enigma of the Arrival and the Afternoon:"

Two shrouded figures turn from each other

in a too-clean plaza. Piazza San Croce,

where the artist, it's said, fell in love with Italy.

Light falls obliquely over a black and white

tiled plaza, illumines a tall ship's looming

sail. A wall divides the scene...

is this a wall of time?

Is time standing still?

Half here, or half gone?

I fall in love with De Chirico's bleak romanticism—
sun falling on a pillared tower; his attempt
to portray the invisible—time crossing
a checker-board floor. But I note the cost.
I tell my son: *Beware the existential, the forfeiture of soul
like the loss of light.* To myself I say, *do not permit
the passage of time to dull the vibrancy of your mind*

though every solstice I feel it binding me,
with my life mid-summer half-blind.

x. *Michelangelo on the Cusp*

And David too is on the edge—
exactly between reflection and action
when the sun slips into position
and he releases the stone from his sling.

The rock strikes exactly right
and the Goliath falls. The world
turns, solstice stills, and as night
comes on, we see it's not the sun

that leaves—it's we who turn from the sun.
The earth's tilt shifts the balance, begins to tip
us away from summer, into the callous
space of winter. But today, the sun at the cusp

seems to pause in its highest position, just as
Michelangelo sculpts David at the cusp of his
decision—same as the moment Michelangelo
releases David from the stone—

the way we release from our bodies,
with split-second precision, our souls.

The sun holds still another day before
its journey back; without fail, I hear
mother's cautioning voice, *we're headed
for dark*. Not the world turning

backward, no, we still move forward,
even as we tour the shadow. The stone
must leave the sling for the world to end
—for the world to end and again begin.

Alló

Somewhere a telephone is ringing.
An ebonite phone from the nineteen-fifties,
its mouth and earpiece sit rocking in the cradle
atop the circular puzzle in which you place
your finger to dial the future. The ringing
continues even as distance, also known
as time, diminishes.

Alló? Alló? . . . the receiver solid and stable
in the hands of the present . . . as the ringing flies
like swallows in and out the bell tower. The river
of speaking flows through the receiver
as a person, you, or I, presently receives it,
catches the current as it gathers its belongings
from the dream of museums and enters

Dante's woods. But we're back home. Someone,
please, pick up the phone.

Reprise

The fields of golden heliopsis (false
sunflower) in their joyful blooming
can't know whether the next moment
brings life or decline, nor can they choose it,

but there must be that point of surrender
when the flower equivalent of decision,
a determination, is made. In Michelangelo's
David, the outcome of success or failure is

possible until the moment of action when the sun
slips into position and David slings his stone.
At solstice, the sun, like a palindrome, begins
its backwards run. The axis shifts the balance

toward winter; we lose summer's sunlit provision.
The earth twirls with its face toward the sun,
then inexorably faces away again. Gather your
flowers. You must make your decision.

Illustrations: Strozzo Strozzi's Design from the Baptistery in Florence, Italy

Author photograph. Scorpio, Sagittarius, Capricorn visible. The palindrome around the sun is barely legible.

A rendering of the inlay from the Institute and Museum of the History of Science:
www.museogalileo.it

Notes

My gratitude to Dr. Andrew S. Becker in the Department of Modern and Classical Languages and Literatures at Virginia Tech University for his enormous help in translating the phrase *"En Giro Torte..."* and reference material which included contextualization of the life and research of Giovanni Villani (ca. 1290 -1348).

Villani discusses Strozzi's design along with the palindrome as a "rare monument." He states that the design references the *"sistema cosmico tolemaico"*—the Ptolemaic cosmic system. But Ptolemy's system had the earth as the center of the universe, not the sun.

Copernicus published his model of heliocentrism in 1543. Villani, living in the early 1300s, might not have noticed that the *"En giro torte"* line suggested the sun was the center of our solar system, or that the image on the floor from the 11th century was depicting this. Villani said, "It was made for astronomy;" suggesting the design's importance as an astronomical clock, marking summer solstice. (It is indeed one of the earliest in Europe.)

Villani's translation, at a time when the archaic language might've been better understood, was: "I, sun with fire, make the circles turn twistedly and I turn too." The "circles," used in Medieval astronomy to indicate a repeating span of time, are likely a reference to the planets orbiting in a circular path.

Veronica Sanitate is the author of *The Palindrome of the Sun* (Finishing Line Press, 2026). Her poetry manuscript *Sun Standing Still* was shortlisted for the Faulkner-Wisdom Creative Writing Competition. A winner of the *First Wednesday* Contest, her work has appeared in *Bear River Review, Poetry in Performance, Writers Reading at Sweetwaters,* as well as in the anthologies *Time Is My Window* (Ed. David Barr) and *A History of Dyers Bay.* She holds an MFA from the University of Southern Maine's Stonecoast Program.

In addition to her creative work, Sanitate serves as Vice President of Ocean Organics Corp. and is a founding director of both the Michigan Collaborative for Mindfulness in Education and *Groundcover News*, a street newspaper focused on homelessness solutions. The seventh child of Italian immigrants, she was born and raised in Detroit and now lives in Ann Arbor, Michigan with her husband. Together, they have raised three children and are enjoying their six grandchildren. As a Reiki Master and Intuitive Healing Practitioner, Sanitate brings a deep interest in the healing arts to her life and work.

www.ingramcontent.com/pod-product-compliance
Lightning Source LLC
Chambersburg PA
CBHW022100080426
42734CB00009B/1432